HOW MY BODY **WORKS**

Senses

Anita Ganeri

Evans Brothers Limited

First published by Evans Brothers Limited in 2006
2a Portman Mansions
Chiltern St
London W1U 6NR

British Library Cataloguing in Publication Data
Ganeri, Anita
Super Senses
      1.Senses and sensation - Juvenile literature
      2. Human physio
   Juvenile literature
   I. Title

ISBN 0 237 53185 2
13-digit ISBN (from 1 January 2007) 978 0 237 53185 0

Credits
Editorial: Louise John
Design: Mark Holt & Big Blu Design
Artworks: Julian Baker
Consultant: Dr M Turner
Photographs: Steve Shott
Production: Jenny Mulvanny

Printed in China by WKT Co. Ltd

Acknowledgements
The author and publisher would like to thank the following
for kind permission to reproduce photographs:

Science Photo Library, p.12 (Professors P.
Motta/Department of Anatomy/University 'La Sapienza',
Rome), p.13 (Department of Clinical Radiology, Salisbury
District Hospital), p.15 (Astrid and Hanns-Frieder Michler),
p.22 (Philippe Plailly/Eurelios).

Photograph on p.11 by Peter Millard. All other
commissioned photography by Steve Shott. Models from
Truly Scrumptious Ltd. With thanks to: Nicole Aurellano,
Nicola and Justin Mooi, Mylton Burdon, Indiana Frankham,
Ariadne Snowden, Courtney Thomas and also Ellen and
Jack Millard. Copyright © Evans Brothers Ltd 2003.

VISIT OUR WEBSITE
Evans
www.evansbooks.co.uk

Contents

Making sense

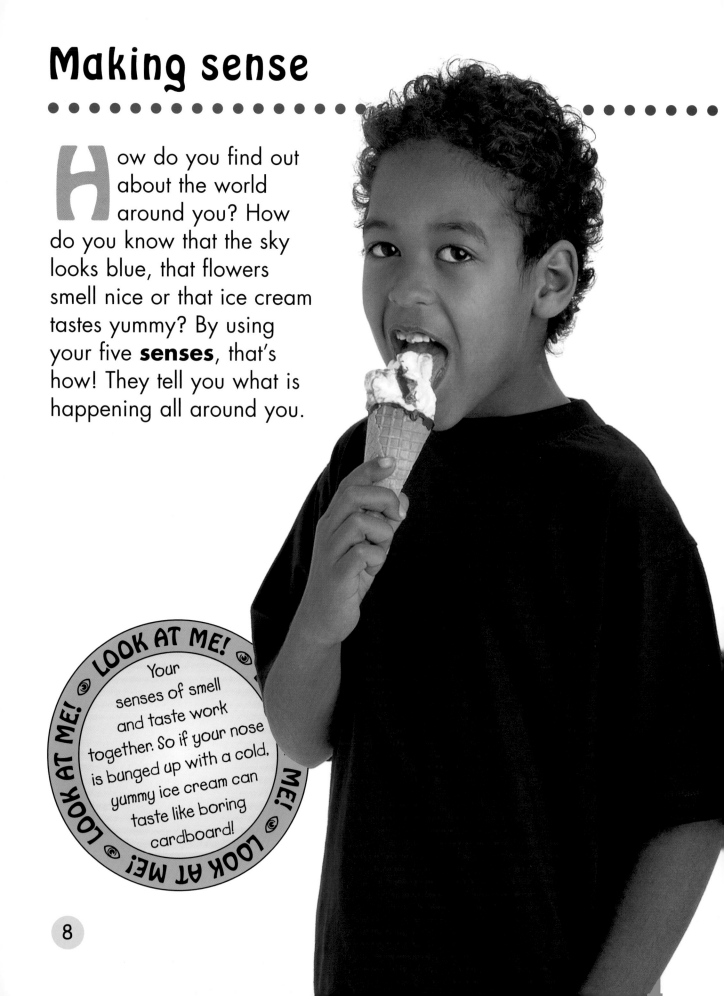

How do you find out about the world around you? How do you know that the sky looks blue, that flowers smell nice or that ice cream tastes yummy? By using your five **senses**, that's how! They tell you what is happening all around you.

LOOK AT ME! Your senses of smell and taste work together. So if your nose is bunged up with a cold, yummy ice cream can taste like boring cardboard!

Your five senses are touching, smelling, hearing, tasting and seeing.

1 You feel things with your skin. It tells you if things are rough or smooth, hot or cold, or painful.

2 You smell things with your nose. That's how you can smell the delicious food you're having for your tea!

3 You hear things with your two ears. They can pick up all sorts of sounds.

4 You taste things with your tongue. It is covered in tiny bumps, called **tastebuds**.

You see things with your eyes. You can see in colour and in black and white.

Messages from outside

Each of your senses is linked to your brain. Your brain is the most important part of your body. It makes sense of what is happening to you. When you read this book, your eyes send messages about the words and pictures to your brain. The messages travel through a network of **nerves**. Your brain sorts them out and tells you what you are seeing. It also tells your fingers to turn the page when you've finished reading!

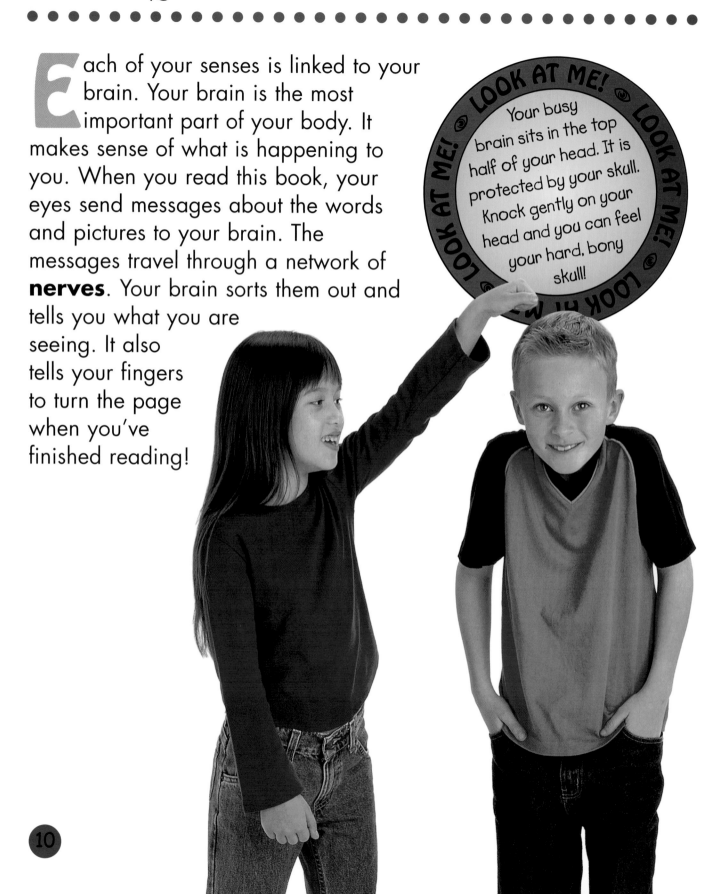

LOOK AT ME! LOOK AT ME! LOOK AT ME!

Your busy brain sits in the top half of your head. It is protected by your skull. Knock gently on your head and you can feel your hard, bony skull!

You have about 100 million nerves running all around your body. Some nerves carry messages from your five senses to your brain. Some carry messages from your brain to your muscles to tell them to move. Others pass messages from one nerve to another. This huge nerve network helps you to find out what is happening outside you. Your brain and your nerves are called your nervous system.

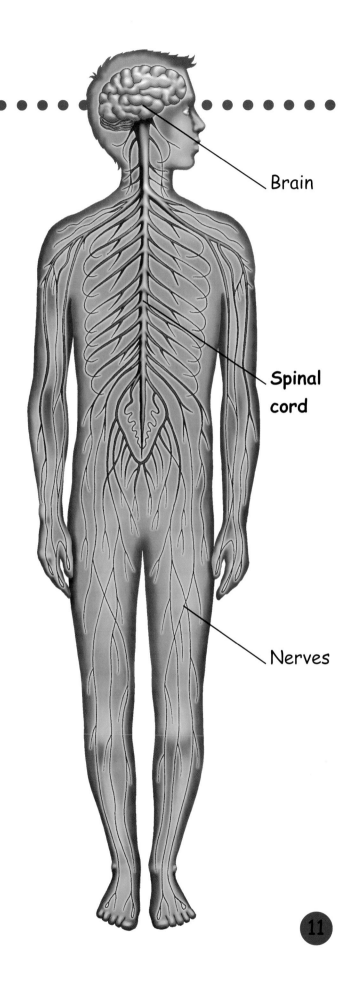

Brain

Spinal cord

Nerves

AMAZING!

Every minute, millions and millions of messages are whizzing around your body.

Eye spy

Look at your eyes in a mirror. Can you see two tiny, black dots in the middle of them? These are your **pupils**. Pupils are really holes which let light go into your eyes. Your eyes need light to see. That's why you can't see very well in the dark.

LOOK AT ME! • LOOK AT ME! • LOOK AT ME! • LOOK AT ME! •

Try munching on a carrot. Carrots can help you to see in the dark. They contain **vitamin A**, which helps the **cells** in your eyes to pick up light.

12

Light bounces off everything you look at and goes into your eyes. Then special nerves in the back of your eyes send messages to your brain and your brain tells you what you are looking at. But the picture that your nerves send is upside down. Your brain has to turn it the right way up.

This is what the different bits of your eyes do:

Your eyeball is made from jelly, to keep your eye the right shape.

The back of your eye is called the retina. This is where the picture forms.

A nerve at the back of your eye carries messages to your brain.

Tiny **lenses** in your eyes focus the light, so the picture you see isn't fuzzy.

The black hole in the middle of your eye is called the pupil.

The white bit at the front of your eye protects the parts behind it.

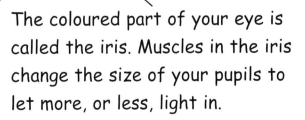

The coloured part of your eye is called the iris. Muscles in the iris change the size of your pupils to let more, or less, light in.

More about eyes

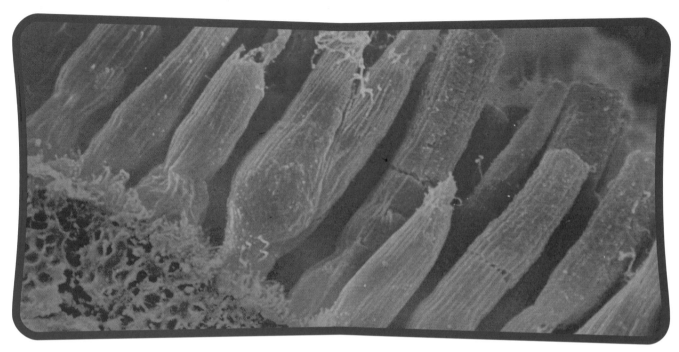

Rod and cone cells, seen under a microscope.

Tiny nerve cells in the back of your eyes pick up the light which shines into them. These nerve cells are called rods and cones. Rods help you to see in black and white and to see in dim light. Cones help you to see in colour. They work best in bright light. That's why it's hard to see bright colours at night.

Some people are **colour blind**. They can't see certain colours properly because their cones don't work very well. They find it hard to tell red and green colours apart.

AMAZING!

Eyes can be different colours – blue, brown, hazel or green. You inherit your eye colour from your parents. What colour are your eyes?

14

Do you wear glasses to help you see clearly? Some people need glasses to help them see close to, or far away. Otherwise, the picture they see looks fuzzy. Glasses are extra lenses. They help the real lenses in your eyes to focus the light that comes into them.

LOOK AT ME! ⊚ LOOK AT ME! ⊚ LOOK AT ME! ⊚ LOOK AT ME! ⊚ LOOK AT ME!

Having two eyes gives you a better all-round picture of things. Try shutting one eye, then the other. Can you notice the difference?

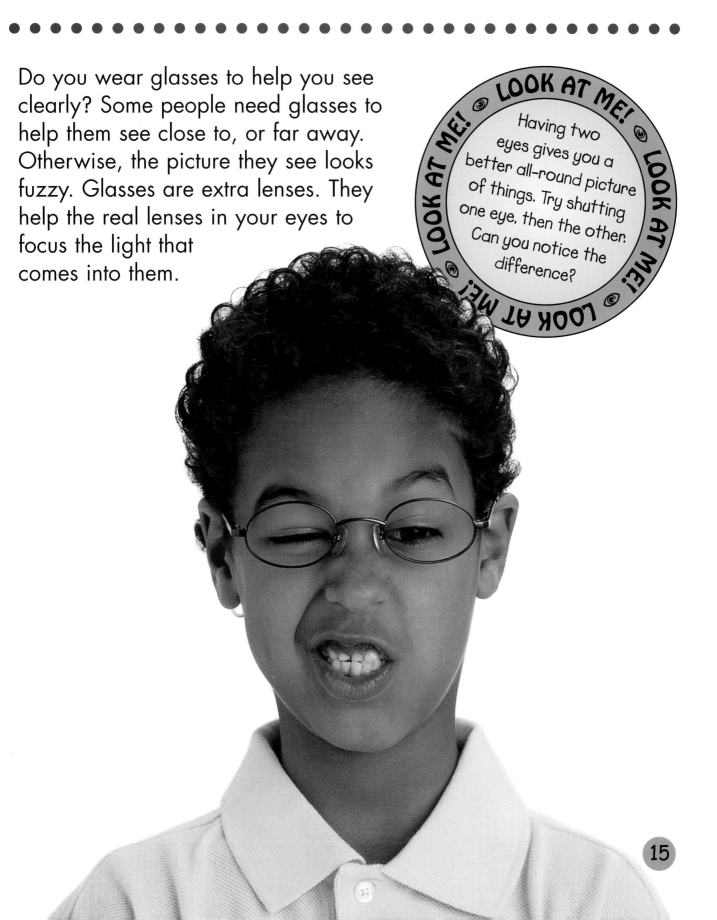

15

Ear, ear

Your ears might look a funny shape but this makes them very useful. They are shaped a bit like funnels to help them catch sounds from the air. Sounds make the air wobble. The sounds go in through your ear hole and inside your head, to the inside parts of your ear that you can't see.

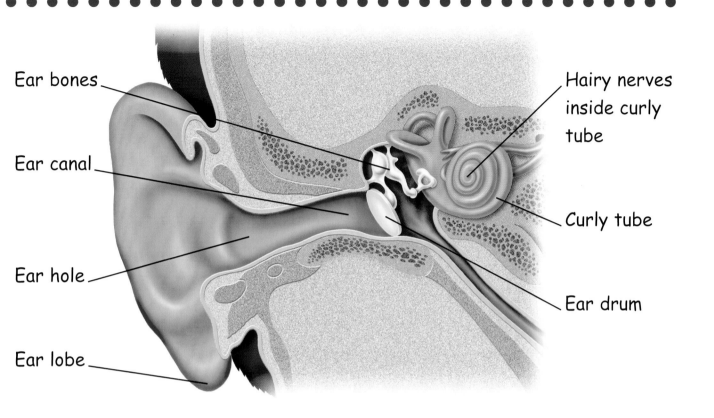

Ear bones

Ear canal

Ear hole

Ear lobe

Hairy nerves inside curly tube

Curly tube

Ear drum

Inside your ear, the sounds go down a tube, called your ear canal. At the end, they hit a bit of thin, tight skin, called your ear drum. The sounds make your ear drum wobble. When your ear drum wobbles, it makes three tiny ear bones wobble, too. The bones send the wobbling deeper into your ears. Next, the wobbling hits a curly tube, which is filled with liquid and hairy nerves. The liquid shakes and pulls on the nerves. They send messages about the sounds to your brain. Then your brain tells you what you can hear.

AMAZING!

The tiny bones inside your ears at the smallest bones in your body. They are about the same size as grains of rice.

More about ears

Why do you think you have two ears? It's because it helps you to tell where sounds are coming from. The sounds hit one of your ears just before the other one, so the wobbles in the first ear are stronger than the wobbles in the second ear.

Your amazing ears can hear sounds as loud as a jet plane or as soft as a person whispering. But if you listen to loud sounds for too long, it can harm your hearing. Your ears can also hear high and low sounds. High sounds make the air wobble very fast. Low sounds make it wobble slowly.

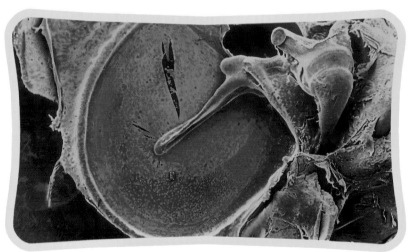

Your ear drum, as seen under a microscope.

Can you spin round very fast without getting dizzy and falling over? Your ears help you to balance. In each ear, you have curly tubes, filled with watery liquid. When you move your head, the liquid sloshes about in the tubes. Special nerves pick up this movement and send messages to your brain. Your brain adjusts the rest of your body to stop you falling over.

LOOK AT ME! LOOK AT ME! LOOK AT ME! LOOK AT ME!

When ballet dancers spin round and round, they keep their eyes on a fixed spot. This stops them feeling dizzy.

What a pong!

Some things smell nice, like a bunch of flowers or a freshly-baked cake. Other things smell terrible, like smelly socks or milk that's gone off. Smells are made from tiny bits which float in the air. Your nose picks up these smells.

LOOK AT ME! ⊚ LOOK AT ME! ⊚ LOOK AT ME! ⊚ LOOK AT ME! ⊚ LOOK AT ME!

Do you wrinkle up or hold your nose when you smell something horrible? This stops air and smells going up your nose.

When you breathe in, smells in the air go up your nose. The smells are too small to see. But special hairy nerves inside your nose soak up the smells and send messages about them to your brain. Then your brain tells you what sort of smell it is.

Sniffing helps smells smell stronger. Usually, when you breathe, you only take in a small gulp of air. But when you sniff hard, you take in a big gulp of air and the smells go straight to your nose nerves.

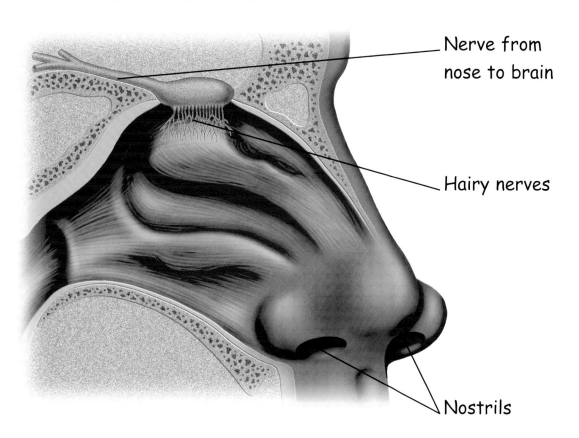

Nerve from nose to brain

Hairy nerves

Nostrils

Tastes good

What's your favourite taste? Do you like sweet things, like yummy ice cream, or salty things, like crunchy crisps? You taste things with your tongue. It's covered in lots of tiny bumps called tastebuds. They send messages along nerves to your brain to tell you what your food tastes like. Your tongue also tells you if your food is hot or cold.

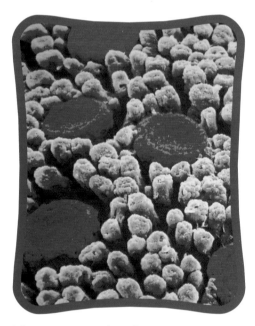

Your tastebuds, seen under a microscope.

LOOK AT ME! LOOK AT ME! LOOK AT ME! LOOK AT ME!

Look in a mirror and stick out your tongue. Can you see the tiny bumps on the surface? These are your taste-buds.

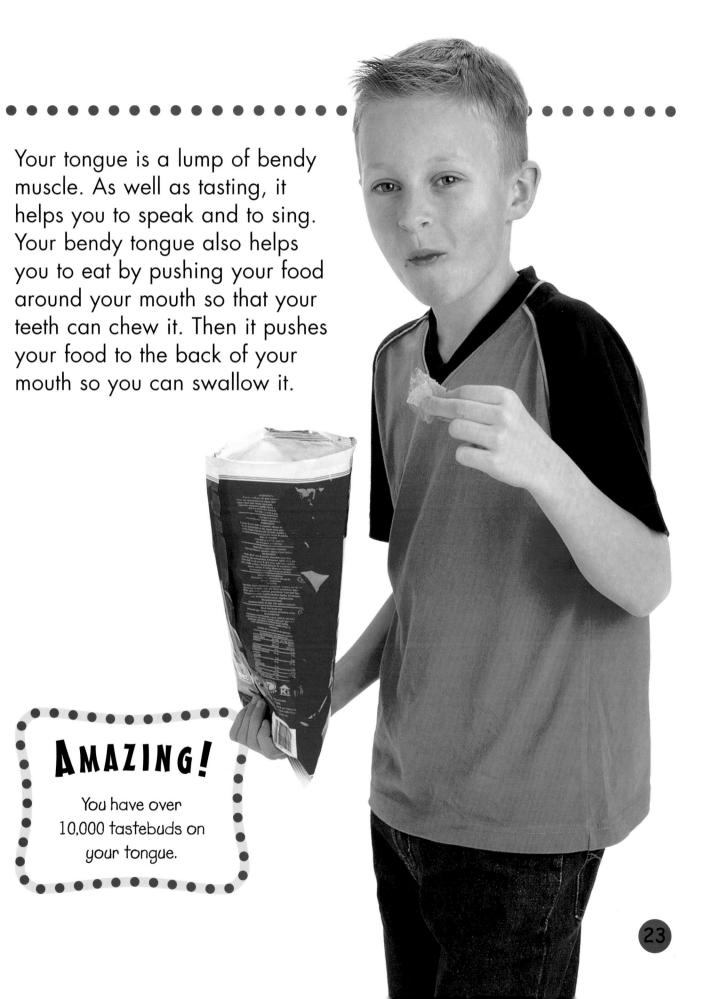

Your tongue is a lump of bendy muscle. As well as tasting, it helps you to speak and to sing. Your bendy tongue also helps you to eat by pushing your food around your mouth so that your teeth can chew it. Then it pushes your food to the back of your mouth so you can swallow it.

AMAZING!

You have over 10,000 tastebuds on your tongue.

Touchy, feely

You touch and feel things with your skin. Your skin touches the things around you. It tells you if things are hot or cold, soft or hard or rough or smooth, or painful.

Your skin covers your whole body. It fits your body perfectly and bends and stretches when you move. It holds your insides in. Packed under your skin are millions of tiny nerves. They send messages to your brain to tell you what you are touching or feeling.

LOOK AT ME!

The skin on your finger tips is very sensitive. That is why stroking a cat feels soft and warm.

The surface of your skin, seen under a microscope.

Every second, nerves in your skin send messages to your brain. But your skin isn't equally **sensitive** all over. In some places, the nerves in the skin are close together and the skin is more sensitive. In other places, they are far apart. Your most sensitive skin is on your fingertips, lips and toes. Your toughest skin is on your back and legs.

More about skin

Apart from feeling and touching, your skin has lots of other important jobs to do. Your skin protects your body from harm. It helps to keep you warm on cold days, and cool on hot days. It quickly mends itself if you get a cut or a scratch. Your skin is also covered in a thin coat of oil. This makes it smooth and waterproof. This is why you don't get soggy when you go swimming!

LOOK AT ME! ⊚ LOOK AT ME! ⊚ LOOK AT ME! ⊚ LOOK AT ME! ⊚ LOOK

Look at your fingertip through a magnifying glass. Can you see a pattern on the skin? This is your fingerprint.

No one else has the same fingerprints as you.

26

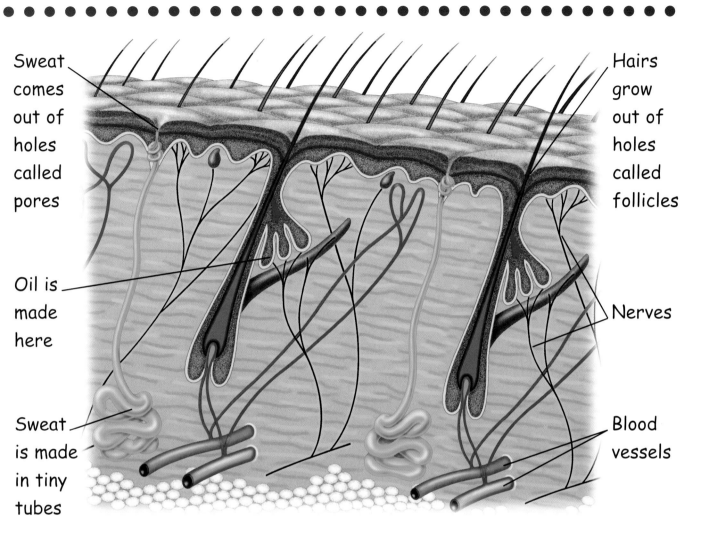

Sweat comes out of holes called pores

Oil is made here

Sweat is made in tiny tubes

Hairs grow out of holes called follicles

Nerves

Blood vessels

In most places, your hard-wearing skin is only as thick as a piece of cardboard. But lots of things happen inside your skin. Hair grows from tiny holes in your skin. Other holes make salty **sweat**. Tiny tubes, called **blood vessels**, bring blood to your skin. Blood brings your skin **oxygen** from the air you breathe, and goodness from the food you eat.

AMAZING!

The thickest skin on your body grows on the soles of your feet. The thinnest skin grows on your delicate eyelids.

27

Glossary

Blood vessels The thin tubes which carry blood around your body.

Cells The tiny building blocks which make up every part of your body.

Colour blind Not able to see certain colours, such as red and green, properly.

Lenses Clear discs inside your eyes which focus light so that you see a clear picture.

Nerves Special cells, which carry messages between your body and your brain. They look like long wires.

Oxygen A gas in the air which you need to breathe to stay alive.

Pupils The black dots in the middle of your eyes. They are actually tiny holes, which let light through.

Senses The way in which your body tells you what is happening around you. Your five senses are touching, smelling, hearing, tasting and seeing.

Sensitive Able to feel or touch things.

Spinal cord The bundle of nerves which runs down your back, inside your spine (backbone).

Sweat A liquid made in your skin which helps to keep you cool on a hot day.

Tastebuds Tiny bumps on your tongue which pick up different flavours in your food.

Vitamins Important substances in your food which your body needs to stay strong and healthy.

Index